Perpetual Flaws

Perpetual Flaws

I have a lifetime to live without you
and I am not ready for that.

memoirsofbilal

i spilled ink to touch your heart.
Sorry, if it pokes your wound.

memoirsofbilal

it's time for us
to lose the knot
that is biding us
suffocatingly.

my sins
no longer compliment
your perpetual flaws.

so much has changed
and years have gone by –
i wonder,
if you're still the same person i met?

do you remember me
as the person you loved?
or have you forgotten me
because you decided
i was not right for you?

do you remember
how madly i was in love with you?

it was months ago
and you never had an idea
on how to respond.

perhaps, you were more scared
to be loved by someone
than to love another soul.

i remember all the times
i confessed my feelings
and you always looked away —
like you do now.

my life was really different then,
but how do i tell you now?
my feelings haven't changed yet.

it felt like the end of the world,
end of my world.

for a long time, i felt i was stuck
while writing a poetry
and there was nothing to rhyme
with '*my love for you*'.

you moved on and i had to walk away.

for a while, i tried to hold on
until i realized you'd already let go.

Perpetual Flaws

i was perfectly intact when you started adoring me,
but your love was only meant to break me.

you didn't leave me with wounds and scars –
you broke me beyond repair.

i struggled for a while
yet strived to put myself together.

i started to collect my broken pieces
but failed because a part of me was missing.

a part that i loved the most,
a part that i had always cherished —
a part i was scared to lose.

i did everything i could to get it back
but with time, i realised
that it would always be missing.

i can never be whole and the missing piece
will always remind me of that.

sometimes, you lose people.
people who promised to stay — walk away,
right in front of your eyes
and there's nothing you could do about it.

as much as you hold onto them,
it hurts until you let go.
and you lose yourself along with them.

sometimes, you lose people
and they say, it's for good.

sometimes, you lose people
you wish you didn't

and sometimes, you pray they stayed.

sometimes, you know the reason
but other times, it is what it is.

our heart breaks
because no one told us
while we were growing up
that love doesn't come with
terms and conditions
that guarantee
forever, always
and no matter what.

i don't understand
why i keep things
that i no longer need.

for example — flower in my book,
a white shirt i probably wouldn't wear,
ripped pair of shoes
and your memories.

why do you come back every time
when i'm close to forgetting you?

why do you have to leave
all the time when
i'm deeply in love with you?

some nights, i walk down the empty street that has dim
lights and broken path.

there is not much to be seen
other than ruined homes
and silent echoes is all i hear.

i don't know much about it
but there's nothing else in this world
other than the street i could relate to.

emptiness, void, darkness and shattered pieces
of everything that once made it beautiful.

i've lost my memory and struggle to remember —
everything, something, anything.
i can't muse on anything but in the back of my mind,
there's a notion of you.
i'm turning the pages of my journal to get to the day
when i had met you for the first time.
i'm trying to recollect all the memories we framed
together.
it hurts – it hurts that i no longer remember how i
confessed my love and what you answered.
i can't summon up what i felt during all the time we
spent together.
i'm exploring every inch of my existence to find the
places i left my broken pieces at, when you choose to
walk away from me.
i'm certain that i still love you — but i want to
reminisce how it felt when the love was reciprocated.
i'm not certain who i'm anymore yet my heart compels
me that it knows you.
i'm not looking for myself anywhere but i can't bear to
afford the loss of our saga.

you were everything i never imagined having,
your love imprisoned me yet i was free.

it was after you let go of me,
i realized what real cage feels like.

i remember you once said to me that you were attracted
to my smile and how you noticed kindness in my eyes
— it was, after a lifetime, i felt i was worthy and i
believed that i deserved to be loved too.

i fell in love with you and hoped that you'd fall in love
with me too. i was scared of losing you and thought
you were scared of losing me, too.

it was later, i realised that you were not in love with me
— all you wanted was someone to take away your
loneliness, someone to fill the emptiness in your heart.

you started breaking me — pieces by pieces; you broke
me beyond repair and all i wanted was to take my heart
out of my chest to prove how much i loved you.
i wonder if it made you happy?
did it make you smile when you looked at me few
months later and saw the broken pieces you created?
did you realise that you were the reason behind my
tired soul?
did you see the disappointment in my eyes?

i remember the last time i asked why you did what you
did to me — all you said was nothing and all my
questions were never answered.

every now and then, i find myself staring at your pictures and think about all the things i fell in love with — your pretty eyes and your beautiful nose. i think of the mark between your fingers and the touch of your hand. it's been a long time since you decided to walk away but i still remember you once said that my hand fit perfectly in yours and you'd never let go of it. that's what you wanted, at least my heart believed you did. i know i should forget you — i must forget you and fall out of love but it's not easy. i mean, if i could, i would but i still hear those promises you made and the words you whispered in my ear. i know, you no longer love me like you said you loved me but i hope you know i loved you when i said i did and your absence never made a difference to it.

have you ever seen someone wearing a pair of shoes
that's ripped at edges?

it's faded all over and there's a crack at the bottom. you
see creases and loose threads. but they wear it anyway
— they wear it all the time.

the pair is messy and embarrassing but they're too
comfortable with it and can't imagine walking around
without the old pair because it's scary to let go.
they never want to let it go.

i hope the love of your life never becomes that old pair
of shoes.

you're beautiful — just like the full moon.
strong,
bright
and illuminating.

i had started to look for you in the times of darkness.
but i didn't realise
how and when, i turned myself into a wolf.

in full moon nights like these — i howl.
and my soul shatters
into pieces when i'm unable to touch
what my whole being loves.

you told me, you left me because you thought you're
not the one i deserve.

and if it's true, i have a few questions that i want
answers from you —
if you're not the one i deserve then why does my heart
carry so much love for you?
if we were not meant to be together, why did our paths
had to cross?
you noticed my fear and insecurities, but why did you
not see that i had finally started to let go of them?
why is it that i showed you where it hurt the most and
you decided to stab me right there?
if you're not the one i deserve, then why do i spend my
nights staring at your photos and my days, embracing
your voice notes?
and after all this, why can i still not convince my heart
that you are a bad person, and that you're not right for
me?
was it really this easy for you to give up on us?

you promised, you wanted my happiness and i always
said you were my happiness but you chose to let it go
by leaving me stranded in the end and deciding for
yourself that i was not your destiny.

the most tragic,
unfortunate
and agonizing
reality is –

i want to tell you
how i feel
but it won't make any difference
to our differences.

i didn't understand what was happening to me until i realised, i was deeply in love with you. all my days — i prayed for us and wished to spend the rest of my life with you. i believed; we would last forever. it scared me, when your love started to fade and i was petrified of what i was going to do once you're gone. i wanted you to know that you were so into me that i was nowhere to be seen in myself. i cannot express how much you meant to me. perhaps, that's why your happiness meant more to me than your love did. i wanted to hold onto you but all you willed was to walk away and that's why i had to let you go. i hope, one day, you look back and see the pieces of my heart you broke, a heart that fails to be fixed. i hope you realise that you broke my heart and damaged your home.

and i was wounded,
and i was bruised,
and i was trying to heal myself,
but you came along.

and you held me by my hands,
and you kissed me on the scars,
and you fell in love with me,
but you said we won't end up together.

and i thought of you,
and i dreamt of you,
and i thought i may fall,
but you assured in the beginning —
you won't catch if i fall.

and you said i make you happy,
and you said you want me now,
and you know there's no happy ending,
even if you decide to catch when i fall.
i am i with a lot of ifs,
you are you with a lot of buts,
and my heart tells me, we can never be us.

i can do nothing but pray
because my heart knows
we're not meant to be.

you don't mean
a lot to me.
just as necessary
for my existence
as similes and metaphor
for a poem.

your touch had given me wounds that made me miss
you yesterday.
the blood in the wounds from yesterday makes me miss
you even more today
and the ache in these wounds will make me miss you
forever.

time will never heal these wounds for i have understood
it,
very clearly.

time will give me clarity, assurance and understanding
of my love that doesn't depend on your presence.
time will only tell me that my love has grown stronger
in your absence.

may you be safe from the love –
that is miserable when absent
and lethal when present.

your love was the solace
i escaped in,
though it's now the emptiness
i choke in.

just stop for a moment – take a pause and think.

think about everything that has happened to you.
think about the secret you have never shared with
anyone,
think about the person who broke your heart
and the friends who betrayed your trust.
think about the people who tried to kill your potential
and think about the times you thought you wouldn't
survive. it is important to think and feel and act through
your emotions.

don't choose to bury your feelings – it doesn't help.
cry if you want to, scream if you feel like.

but feel. and reflect.

if it didn't happen to you, you wouldn't have learnt to
say no to things you want but don't need.
if someone hadn't broken your heart you wouldn't have
learnt to respect emotions. in fact, you wouldn't have
become the person that you are today.

look at yourself once again –
did you notice your smile? it has become more
beautiful.
can you see your tears are now crystal?
do you feel your golden heart?
are you falling deeper in love with yourself?

i looked at my phone — waiting to see your name
popping up in my notification, hoping that you'd be the
first one to wish me.
before that night, i had no idea that an event could
make so much of a difference — even though you told
me the next day you didn't forget, i had realised that i
wasn't as important as i thought i was — perhaps,
that's when i had lost you for the first time.
few days later, we had gotten into a fight — all i know
is that it was my mistake but all it proved to me was
that your ego meant more to you than the love you said
you had in you.
i assumed, that was it — i had broken your heart but
you wrecked my soul when i found out that you'd been
lying to me and i lost you one more time.
on our last call — you said you love me but your
actions recited a completely different story.
i had lost all hope until tonight when i picked up my
phone to dial your number and my heart refused
because i no longer love you — i love the person i
thought you were.

i felt a void.
during all this time apart — i had only hoped to hear
from you on this day.
it was only a minute — sixty more second to go.
i prayed for something, a little too special and forgot
that things like fairy tale don't happen to me.
everyone around started the countdown.
at 10, i looked at the door.
and at 9, i believed it would open
but at 8 — i ended up a little disappointed.
there was nothing i could do at 7
and at 6, i accepted the truth.
who would have thought?
that my smile was fake at 5
and my hands started to shiver at 4.
at 3, i closed my eyes
and your face flashed at 2.
everyone cheered at 1
and before i could blow out the candle,
my tears snuffed it off.

somewhere between our conversations, i had started to
hope for something more than usual — your likes on
my posts, your name popping up in my notifications
and calls had started to bring smile on my face. i found
you when i wasn't looking for anyone and perhaps,
that's why being with you was becoming a part of me. i
wanted to know a lot about you — your favourite color
or if you like to watch the sunset more than the color of
sky as the sun rises. i wanted to see how your eyes
shine when the moon casts it's light on your face and
we would see the stars at night. i am unsure if the
timing wasn't right or if what i felt wasn't real but i
guess what we had didn't mean to last — you wanted
me to stay and i thought we could go on forever but i'm
glad we had our own little infinity.

the saddest part is not crying during last one third of the
night, it not pouring your heart out — it's finally giving
up. it's finally giving up on your dreams, wishes and
desires because you come to terms that you never
deserve any of it. the saddest part is that fake hope —
the hope that's given to people when they lose
something. the cruellest part is the hope that tells
there's something better. why do we always talk about
something better that is to come? why do we not talk
about the good we've lost? what if someone had
already lost a good and is now letting go of the better?
the saddest part is realising that you never deserved the
good you had lost and you were not good enough for
what you thought was your better.

i wonder what goes through your mind when you hear
my name?
does your heart drop for a moment just like my throat
chokes?
does it remind you of my love and care?
do you ever think about our conversations and my
endless affection?
i wonder if there's something that reminds you of what
we once were –
how you broke my heart in pieces and ripped my soul
apart?
i hope one day, when you hear my name — you
remember how much i tried to hold on, though you'd
effortlessly let go.

it's ironic how i fail every time when i attempt to tell
the world how much i love you — when i can't find
words to frame a poetry about your eyes.

i could waffle for days yet flunk to express the taste of
your divine lips and to find a perfect metaphor for your
fleecy hair.

i don't know how to express what i felt when i sat next
to you and the symphonies i heard when you talked.

i knew it — i knew you would leave me speechless
when i first saw you but you chose to leave me lifeless
when you decided to abandon me.

i don't miss you.
but i miss how beautifully you used to break me —
pieces by pieces.
each day.
if i must tell what i miss the most — it's the way i
adored your ignorance and how you ignored my
presence. i miss how i breathed every second to grab
your attention.
i am not sure but did you ever feel my helplessness?
love isn't supposed to do that.
i miss whatever it was i had let you do to me and it's
awfully sad that you'd never understand what you
meant to me.
you didn't deserve me but i miss how cruelly you
owned me.

Perpetual Flaws

i wish you could come back.
i wish i could meet you once again.

i remember the spark in your eyes
when you used to talk about the things
you were passionate about.

i still have flashes of your smiling face
and sometimes, i hear the echoes
of your laughter.

it hurts that you're nowhere to be found
and i think i have forgotten you.

i wish we get to meet again and
i hope, on that day, you remember me.

Perpetual Flaws

i want to capture you in my camera. i want to seize the
smirk on your face and record the spark in your eyes
when you smile — a smile that enlightens my soul. i
want to photograph your vulnerability when you're are
lost in your thoughts and forget about the world. you
captivate me, when you scratch your nose while
listening to stories. i want to keep you in my memories
so that one day i could look back and think about the
love that i wish was mine.

never in a million year did i think that i'd pray to have
someone like i do for you.

i wish you knew how much your smile means to me
and how difficult are my days because you're no longer
around.

i wish you could see through my mind and see what
goes in, ever since you left.

i wish i could pour my heart out to you.

every night i wonder why it has to be the way it is.

and on one of these nights when i want to give up on
myself – i pray you'd come back and tell me that you
failed to give up on me.

we are scared of pricks,
but it's actually rose
that kills us.

when i look at your photographs —
my heart sinks
and i feel knots in my stomach
because i miss you.

it hurts that we've become strangers
and our feelings are buried
in a grave
nobody puts flowers on.

when the pieces of your love puzzle don't fit together
anymore — trust me, they've started to connect
somewhere else.

if you stay –
i'd lose myself.

and if you don't,
i'd lose everything.

either way, i lose.

i had lost all hope, i believed i wouldn't survive but
look — i have gotten better. i'm not disconcerted
anymore with what seemed real to me doesn't exist
now. i no longer deny the fact that you really have
gone. it's not the point where i could say that i'm
happy, but i'm not sad either. i've finally faced my fear
— fear of losing you. you'd be happy to know that i'm
stronger now, as you had always wanted to see —
never did i anticipate the price i'd have to pay. and this
all doesn't mean that i've forgotten you. i miss you; i
truly do but it's not the kind of missing that hurts. since
you left, i'm often told — "when one door closes,
another opens" and i'm certain that it happens but my
heart doesn't want any door to open if you're not
coming in from that.

my heart is like a baby — for it believed in all your lies. i remember when i saw you for the first time, i knew you were going to matter and my heart was certain that we were not meant to be but i convinced myself that you are special.

do you remember the first time we went out? deep down, i knew it was casual but when you called it 'a date' — my little heart believed it. do you remember the first time i found out you that you were not in love with me? or you remember the last time i saw you — you were in bed with someone else. all that my little heart wanted was to die, for it did everything but you couldn't stay in it, you couldn't make my heart, your home.

but i convinced my heart that it was not its fault — my heart deserves all the happiness in the world, i was less fortunate and you know what, it believed. you kept on calling and apologizing, days on end — i stopped responding to your texts and it was not because i was broken or upset, i mean i was but i had to lie to my heart. every morning, my heart has felt the text messages you sent and it had come to the terms that it was not you; it was me who stopped responding and walked out of a beautiful love story. you know, my heart is like a little baby, for it easily believes all the lies.

Perpetual Flaws

i like to think about you
and wonder, what would happen
if you found out little secrets about me?

would your heart melt if you found out
that i still eat your favourite flavour of ice-cream?

all i wanted for you was happiness –
would you come back if you found out that
i really did everything to make you happy.

you are my 11:11 wish and a falling star whisper
and i wonder if you miss me on full moon nights.

some days, i gather courage to go to all the places we
used to hang out at and hope that you might walk down
our memory lane too.

some days, i like to think more about you and
wonder what would happen if you found out
that i am still in love with you?

this.
whatever this is between us — it is not love.
it's the idea of love that we're in love with.

your presence does not make my heart race
nor your absence affects me.

i know you love me the way anyone
would want to be loved,
but how do i reciprocate it now?

for i once believed in this four-letter word 'love',
in the end was nothing more than a reflection
of 'lies' and 'gone'.

now i understand why storms
are named after people —

i was hit by one.

there were no warnings
and no red alert,
it came from nowhere
and destroyed me.

it was causing harm to my soul
and i couldn't stop letting it in —
i embraced it, instead.

little did i know, it was a storm.
it had to pass,
it had to go somewhere else,
to some other place.

i keep waiting for your texts and calls. i keep waiting to hear your voice and telling me that you're sorry. i keep waiting for you to scream at me and tell me that i was wrong too — i keep waiting for you to come and tell me that i was hurting you, too. i don't know why, but i keep on hoping that one day, you would. you would come and tell me that you still love me and you would do anything that it may take for us to work again. i don't trust you but i keep on hoping that you would come back and give me a reason to. i keep waiting for you to come and compel my heart that it still loves you.

Perpetual Flaws

when i fell in love with you —
i promised myself,
that your happiness would be
more important to me than my own.

and i think that's what the hardest vow
i ever had to keep
since i realised, i wasn't your happiness.

it was like, i had to break my own heart
and take away my happiness
to let you have yours.

i really loved
and i hope you trust me
when i say this –
i never wanted to leave you.

every second without you feels longer than a day and
with each passing day - i wonder where i went wrong. i
don't know if i loved you right, but there is no right
way to love; especially when the person you love
becomes your world. every dream i dreamt, meant
nothing to you. all our days, good or bad, are over.
forgotten. i hope you're happy and you never have to
feel anything close to the pain and agony you left me
in. you were not someone i loved back then; you were
my everything - my more. the emptiness in my heart,
where you once lived, can never be fulfilled by anyone
else. as much as i need you, you want me no more and i
think that's what i'm going to live with - counting days
and marking calendar.

on some nights, when i'm not able to sleep — i think about you. or perhaps, i can't sleep because i think about you. most of the nights, i cry and reminisce memories of everything that we used to be. there're days when i hope that you would call and by the night all the pieces of my broken heart shatter on the ground — a little disappointed. i don't know why life works the way it does and i still can't figure out your purpose in my life but i really want you to know that you're someone i'd trade my everything to be with. i still pray for you and i hope, on some night — you'd at least think about us.

i miss how you used to love me. i miss your presence
— those random calls and late-night text messages
about the things that didn't really matter but we would
talk just for the sake of talking. above all, i miss your
stories and the touch of your hand on mine. i miss
going out with you to try new things, things i wouldn't
have done if it weren't for you. and if i were to tell the
world what i miss the most? it's loving you with all my
heart and trusting you wouldn't break it.

if your heart is weak enough
to easily fall in love
with things and people –

be strong enough to believe
that these will be taken
away from you.

i was broken before i met you and instead of getting
hurt from my pieces, you started fixing me — your love
started mending my heart. i told you i was scared of
letting you in, then i always mentioned i was afraid of
not being with you. your promises and what i had seen
in your eyes let me let go of that fear.

they say love is like jumping from the cliff and it feels
like flying, that's true — i was flying in love with you
and everything seemed beautiful. i could touch the sky
and my world was shining like the moon.

and one day, you decided to cut my wings. you
promised you'd never hurt me and you vowed to stay
— so why can't i see you around? why is it that the
memories we created and the life we imagined to live
haunts me now? i was broken before i met you and the
distance between us is tearing me apart.

i promised myself to love you when you think no one
else could — to care for you, to be there for you. above
everything, i promised myself to find whatever it takes
for you to be happy. little did i know, the happiness you
craved for doesn't lie with me. you said, you wanted to
leave; as much as i wanted to hold on — your eyes told
me you wanted to let go. i am happy that you're happy
but it hurts too much to love someone who doesn't
want to be with you.

i wanted to tell you that it hurts, loving you hurts.
instead, i walked away - i walked as far as i could. at
times, i was tired but i had already come too far so i
couldn't find you when i looked back. i am sorry for
letting you go - it wasn't easy and i want to thank you
for coming into my life - you taught me how to love. i
miss you and it's saddening that there is nothing i can
do for you to fall in love with me. i know this for sure,
and i want you to know that too – you're the best thing
to have happened to me even though i was hurt in the
end. i hope you fall in love and i pray that the person
you fall in love with, choose to love you with the same
passion that i do.

sometimes in life,
we are so scared
that we take a pause.

because one step forward
means ten steps away
from something
that we have lost.

love, that controls your fragile heart for days — ends
up as pain that rules your life for months.

you can keep your head high,
stay strong
or fake a smile —

the end of the day craves home.

but how worthless is my "love",
without your "too".

Perpetual Flaws

i love you
more than any other person ever will
and i truly wish you knew –
you're the only one i truly loved
and always will.
it hurts that you don't look at me
the way i look at you,
so, i keep myself away.
but you're never away from my thoughts
and you'll never be forgotten in my *duas*.

i've been meaning to tell you that i'm in love with you,
for a while now. you may ask – how is that possible
since we didn't spend much time together but the
proximity of someone's love cannot be determined by
how much time they have had together. i think about
you all the time.

thought of losing you has become my worst nightmare
and it scares me because i don't have a place in your
dreams. i love you and i love hearing your stories but as
much as i get to know you, it kills a part of me because
i don't see myself in your conversations. it's not that i
didn't love anyone before – it's just that i've never
fallen in love like this - a love to redefine my soul.

i love you and i know you're not mine to keep,
i love you and i know you cannot be with me,
i love you and i know you will never love me
like i love you but you must know that i love you,
more than i thought i was capable of
and more than you think you deserve.

i will not say that no one could love you like i would
but no one will breathe you like i do.

i look at myself and fail to understand how is it possible
for an ordinary person like me to love someone,
deeply?
i remember how you used to love me – i don't know if
you love me now but i won't deny that once you did —
more than i loved you.
i have no idea if our love was wrong or timing wasn't
perfect and i often wonder why did our paths crossed if
we had to end up like this.
i pretend that my breaths are not heavier without you
and i believe you'd leave everything and come back to
me, one day.

all i want you to know is that i really loved you then
and i hope you know; i haven't stopped since.

you don't have to say anything — you don't have to tell
anyone that i was once a best friend you shared your
dark deepest secrets with. you will never have to let
anyone know that i was the one who was there with you
when no one was. please never tell anyone that i'm the
one you failed to replace and the one whose hands fit
perfectly to yours but you had let go of it all very
easily, someone who loved you more than anyone else
ever could. i beg you not to tell anyone that i'm the one
you broke into pieces and never returned when i was
collecting my shattered pieces. i've kept my love as a
secret and this is what you must do – don't tell anyone
about the love that we had taken to the moon.

i don't know
much about love –
except it's only a person,
who feels like home.

"what do i mean to you?", you asked.

i don't think you will fully understand my answer but
here you go — you're a poetry that i'm afraid to write,
you're a song that i want to sing and you're a meaning
that i want to add to my life.

"why do i never answer your questions?" you say.

i don't know if it's fair to say but you're one of the
most beautiful things to have happened to me and good
things like you don't happen to me. if i tell you what
you mean to me, i'm afraid you'll end up hurting me.

if you found out why i never answer your questions,
i'm scared i'll end up breaking your heart.

i'm falling in love with you — with all that you do to
me.
i'm falling in love with the way you look at me and
your smile.
i'm falling in love with how you pretend to sleep in my
arms
and hug me tightly when i kiss you on your forehead.
i'm falling in love with the mark on your hand
and how you hold me when i say i've to leave.

i'm falling in love with the fragrance you wear
and the colour that suit you.

i'm falling in love with the look in your eyes.

i'm falling in love with the way you've made a home
in my heart and how you promise to stay.

i'm falling in love with all the things i'll never tell you
and with all i'm yet to find.

i'm falling in love with everything you think
is not special about you
and something i'm a little scared to confess.

have you ever had a moment when you are broken but
you can't break down?
when you feel lonely, even when you're surrounded by
people — you put a smile on.

it's difficult because everyone can see that you're
talking yet nobody understands what you're trying to
say.
and you carry on, hiding all that you're suffering from?

"i love you, more", that's what you used to tell me and
for a long time, infact, each time you'd say it — i
believed you. i mean how could i not?
if you didn't love me then why would your name
appear in my phone notifications the most? how can i
say you didn't love me when my heart felt at peace
when i heard your voice and you said those words to
me over calls? those hugs and the way you smiled
every time we would meet? do you remember any of
that?

"i know you love me more and you'd never leave me",
that's what i used to reply because my heart trusted you
with it.

i can't recall what i felt when i first met you but i
remember our last meeting — i could feel you leaving
me, i read it in your eyes but it made the least sense of
all because all the time you said you love me, i felt it
and when you said you can't keep up anymore i
realised you don't anymore.

for a second, my heart dropped.
over all this time, i had been thinking how it would feel
to see you with someone new. i will not lie — it hurt
me. and it still hits me in the middle of the nights.
sometimes, i wonder what else i could have done for
you. but for my love — i am at peace.
you are happy, so what else should matter?
that is all i prayed for. i do not want anyone to think
that i am sad — i have a good life and i am blessed
with things and people that i am grateful for.
every second reminds me why i should love myself
before i love someone else.
this is what you were supposed to do — perhaps, that is
why you had to break my heart.

i saw a reflection of someone in the mirror — face covered in tears, soul in blood.

"why are you doing this to yourself?", i asked.

"i promise, i tried to let go", it said.

i want to run away from you — from the pain your presence is causing. i have no idea how to, i want to say goodbye and walk away from all the hurt and lies. i want to forget all the promises you can't keep and all the love that means nothing to you. i want to let go, but i'm not sure why is it so difficult to move on from you.

it's been a year since we met for the first time and it feels as if it was yesterday. my hand was in your hand and your head was on my shoulder. i was embracing the birthmark on your hand and you were promising me 'forever'. i remember i had always told you not to make promises you wouldn't keep and 'i want you, that's it', you would reply. you wanted me to crave you more than i wanted my books and i never stopped loving you ever since. it's been a year and it feels as if it was yesterday when you were madly in love with me. some nights, i forget that we had ever broken up and i hope i would get your text when i wake up next day.

it's not you, it's me. i don't know how else to put it
down — i haven't stopped loving you but someone else
has started to take over my heart. i reminisce all the
nights we spent together, but i only wake up to spend
my mornings with someone else now. it's not you, it's
me. i loved you for who you're but i'm falling in love
with someone who's changed me and made me this
person that i've become. i don't know how else to put it
down. i wish we could go back and i would change my
ways to have never met anyone else other than you. i
understand your silence and i feel your pain because
you're in love with someone who no longer loves you
and i'm in love with someone who may never love me.

you know this person who left you — this person left
you for a reason and there's nothing in this world you
could've done differently for this person to stay
because if this person is meant to stay somewhere —
it's in the past and past is past for some inexplicable
reasons. it happened and now it's gone, so shift your
focus and stop trying to fix what's broken — it'll
always have scars.

"the truth is...", i said, *"we all fake promises."*

i thought to myself about those days when you promised to stay by my side forever and the nights, i confessed i'd die if you leave.

"your forever is over", i sighed.

"i'm still breathing."

i dreamt of you, last night. i met you in my dream. i remember, i held your hand and looked you in the eyes but i'm afraid — they seemed clueless and your smile wasn't serene. your arms had always been my home but the hug last night screamed 'goodbye'. i can easily recall how your hand slipped through mine and later, you faded like you were never there. i promise, i saw you in my dream and it feels, you visited to say that we're not meant to be.

you popped up in 'people you may know' today when i logged in to my facebook account. at first, i felt knots in my stomach but something inside of me asked to click on your name. i'm sure your profile picture was taken when you were bored. i wanted to press the like button, i loved it so much. instead, i scrolled down. i noticed your first crush is added to your friends list and your favourite quote isn't heart-breaking at all. i stared at your date of birth for so long and wondered about the days we would celebrate and those forgotten promises. it's saddening that the person who saw each scar on my soul has ended up in that list. facebook thinks i may get to know you, but the truth is i don't know anyone the way i know you.

i know you loved me — but you loved me like
the favourite toy from your childhood. you'd always
adored me; told me i was your favourite and kept me
safely on the shelf. but i wanted to be loved like the
toys you spend most time with and you give your
attention to. i tried all that i was capable of but i
couldn't get it, so i started to break down. i started to
fall down from the shelf and i loved how you always
fixed me. i can never forget how i'd fallen down the
shelf time and time again and broke into pieces —
you'd always picked up my pieces and kept me back on
the shelf. you'd always told me that you loved me the
most but i couldn't feel it. i wanted to be your toy to
play with but you always played with me when you
were bored by other toys. so, i decided to break down
one last time — but this time, before you'd even tried
to pick up my pieces, i cut your hand and let you bleed.
because i have realized that the pain you feel now will
save you from the heartache later. and i let my pieces
remain broken because i am tired of waiting for you on
the shelf.

"that's the irony in love", i said. "someone can be your everything, yet doesn't belong to you."

i pray for you my love – i pray for you all the good
things in life; i hope you never have to pay the price for
these tears in my eyes. you never have to see the day
when you're choking with words and there's no one to
listen; when you're down in the valley of sorrow and
have no one to lift you up. i pray you never have to live
a day when the depth of emptiness in your chest can't
be measured. i pray your heart never chooses the wrong
person like mine did.

"what went wrong between us?" he asked as she sat across the table in the same café, where they had met for the first time.

"i wish i had an answer", she replied. *"it wasn't like you left me in the middle of a road or we stopped talking. we just drifted apart. you loved me, my heart felt it, but it faded in the end."* a tear fell down her cheek as she continued, *"you were always around me physically, but i could no longer see us together."*

he cupped her face between his hands and kissed her on her forehead — *"do you still love me?"*
"i do", she confessed. *"all this time you were away, i was always told that you would regret leaving me and you may decide to come back."*

"and i am back", he smiled and held her hand. *"for the love you have for me — i want to be yours."*

she pushed him away with tears in her eyes, *"this scares me. i want to love you till the end of time — but i don't want you to break me."*

you touched my heart,
the moment when my name
touched your lips.

at first, i tried to convince myself that i wasn't falling in love with you but the more i walked away from you, i could feel myself falling in love with you. and later, my world started to change and i found myself waiting to hear every wise word that you say. at first, i thought that you could be everything i wanted but the more i thought about it, i realised i am not the one you needed.

i woke up this morning thinking of you or i must say, i couldn't sleep for nights because of you. i find it strange that there was a time when we talked to each other for hours and now, when we have so much to say — we are short of words. i have been praying that you'd wish for me, one day. i hope you'd want to be mine like i promised to be yours. i can't figure out why things happened the way they did and you chose someone else over me. i still pray like i always do — not now but maybe one day, you'll love me, like you used to.

it's been a while and i no longer miss you. i no longer miss your calls and texts. my arms don't long to hold you. i don't crave your presence and your dreams don't haunt me at night. i don't miss you. but i miss us. i miss what we could have been. i miss you looking into my eyes and promising me a forever. i miss holding you and embracing the birthmark on your hand and telling you how much i love it. sometimes, i wonder what went wrong between us — we had become inseparable and like once you said, your hand fit perfectly to mine. sometimes, i wish i should've held you tighter when you wanted me to let go. i don't miss you but i miss what we could have been.

i don't know where it started and i have no idea how i fell for you — perhaps, it was your smile or your pretty eyes. i'm not sure but i think i fell for you because my name sounded beautiful on your lips. i still remember everyone could tell how much i was in love with you and we both know i could've loved even more only if you'd let me.

i saw you with someone new but i still hope you haven't forgotten me because you're the only one i truly remember and there's never been a day since you left that i didn't think about you. i can't seem to figure out how you could be with someone who isn't me and did your heart not stop beating when you looked into someone else's eyes and promised forever like you looked into mine? the sun doesn't seem brighter to me and the rain never washes my sadness away because ever since you left, my life is as dark as the road i first confessed my feelings at.

i hope he notices your face — your eyes, your perfect
nose and how you raise your eyebrows when you smile.
i hope he tells you how beautiful you are, each day
because you deserve it and i didn't tell you that enough.
i don't care if he loves you like i did, but i hope he
won't break your heart like you broke mine. i hope he
puts your feelings first and treat you with love, care and
loyalty. above everything, i hope you're happy with
him now — the happiness that you couldn't find in my
presence. i remember how i fell in love with you and
there is nothing in this world i could do to make you
fall in love with me. but i promise, if ever, he breaks
your heart — know that i'm here. if ever, he stops
writing to you — know that i'm writing about you. if
ever, he falls out of love with you — know that i'm still
in love with you.

love, for me, was not what i thought it would be. it was
absolutely not what i'd known — i didn't hear violin
and there were no flowers. i felt butterflies, but in a
way that they were screaming inside of me. i had hopes
— i'd always believed it would be beautiful, turned out,
it was beautifully ugly. i had forgotten happiness and
lost my way to home.

i thought it was the end — it was the end of it. it was
the moment when i lost you. little did i know i had to
lose you more than once. you think i lost you over the
last text messages we exchanged, but it was not it. i lost
you the next morning again when your name no longer
appeared on my phone screen. i lost you once more
when my friend said my eyes have lost their shine and i
lost you one more time when i picked up my phone to
dial your number until i realised that my love was
suffocating you and you wanted to breathe. i lose you
every time i miss you and realise that you don't miss
me at all.

i'm learning to remind myself that things have changed.
i still sleep on the same bed, under the same roof with
the same pillow but nothing feels familiar. the sky
looks empty and full moon nights are only agonized.
the tree i confessed my love under, has gotten old and
its leaves are falling during this autumn. my days are
restless and nights, sleepless. my ears yearn for your
voice and my hands long for you. i'm trying to
convince myself that you held my heart because you
wanted a toy to play with and i pray you never have to
pay for this broken toy.

i loved you — more than i thought my heart was capable of but you chose every other thing over me. i did everything i possibly could to express my love but you looked for others who never cared. i won't lie through this one; it took me countless days to learn to breathe again and sleepless nights to dream a new world. it's saddening that i made you my poetry, turned out you never wanted me to be a part of your prose.

if i were to tell you what i fell in love with –
it would be a million things followed by you.
number one, the look in your eyes;
number two, the smile on your face;
number three, the sound of my name on your lips.
you once told me that people love your nose,
but i fell in love with the crinkle on it.
you said you never liked the way you walk,
but for me – it's no less than a framed poetry.
if i were to showcase who resides in my heart –
it would be you followed by everything you made me
fall in love with.
number one, people i haven't met;
number two, culture i was never a part of;
number three, all the things i am becoming.
i wish i confessed my love long before you left –
perhaps, you hadn't gone at all.

don't look at me like you look at me,
i looked at someone like you look at me.

don't say what you say to me,
i said it someone like you say it to me.

don't pray for me like you pray for me,
i prayed for someone like you pray for me.

don't dream of me like you dream of me,
i dreamed of someone like you dream of me.

don't wait for me like you wait for me,
i waited for someone like you wait for me.

don't feel for me what you feel for me,
i felt for someone like you feel for me.

don't love me like you love me,
i loved someone like you love me.

you don't know what it does in the end,
because i had let someone do that to me.

the worst part about being hurt is –
you know you're breaking
yet you can't define pain.

i pray
you never have to say
'once upon a time'
with an aching heart.

if tears could bring back the lost love
i wouldn't be sleeping on a drenched pillow.

how do i mention you in my poetry?
when my character no longer
exists in your book.

i don't know why
but i couldn't find words
to describe my love for you.

i don't know why
but i can't find words
to describe the pain
and agony you left me in.

heartbreak is not just a word.
it's a torture, it's torment, pain and affliction.

it's not visible physically – it's a mental suffering.

and obviously not just a phase of life.
it's an end of the character you've been playing in your
life.

how can i be fine knowing
that you were watching
the sunrise with someone
who isn't me?

tell me,
how can i be fine
when you belong to someone
who is not me?

thank you so much
for helping me understand
what it's like to risk,

                    to smile,

     to live,
to love,

                          to
                     hope,

        to wait,
             to cry,
        to gasp,

                        to die.

"what are you looking at?", i was asked.

"colours", i confessed. *"colours of life and how fast they change."*
"what do you mean? what is the colour of life?"

"it was gold. i remember i sat here on the same spot and watched the sunrise with someone who promised to stay."

"okay, then?" another question popped up. *"it turned black – i didn't know how, but i came here and i couldn't look at the same view. i tried but it was too scary to be looked at."*

"are you still scared?"

"fearless."

"and what is the colour of life now?"

"it was blue until you came along."

"what does it mean? do you love me?"

i don't know if this is love because the last time i was here, i used the same word to express this emotion. if that was love, this isn't – it's something beyond.

"does it mean your life is red? the colour of love."

"it's white – i am at peace."

what else my existence be called now –
but your forgotten promise.

we only fall in love once
then we fall in love
to forget the one.

it's unfair to yourself
when you're planning
your fairy tale
with a happy ending –
alone.

love is not blind.
yes,
love is not blind.

i am sure there have been moment when you did
something for someone who's special to you,
something you wouldn't have done if it wasn't for this
person and later blamed it on love.

but here's the truth –
it is not love – it is lust, it is obsession, it is jealousy
and it is fear that is blind.

love open your eyes to real world.
it gives you clarity
and changes your purpose

it is the fear of losing love that makes you blind.

love is not blind.
the world, unless touched by love
is blind.

dear daddy,

you had always taught me to be strong,
brave and honest.

i still remember the bed time stories you'd read
and the lessons to me to make me loving,
patient and kind.

you had done so much for me throughout your time,
made me the person i am today and taught me
everything about life.

but my dear father you've failed
as you never taught me how to cope
with your loss.
you'd never let me cry
and always wiped my tears.

your embrace would lessen my fear
why can't you come back?
and save your baby dear.

you called,
said hi!

followed by the goodbye.

you did everything but *stay.*

i know you don't love me anymore
and won't come back to me ever.

but i want to be overwhelmed –
experiencing pain,

                            once again.

i want to be scared to lose someone
and it's my deepest
most sincere wish
that i want to be broken
by you.

one more time,
one more time
and one more time…

some words mean nothing,
if not come from the one
that means everything.

some nights
when it's *tahajjud* –
i pray for you
and i hope
you pray for me too.

a person who wakes up in the middle of a night soaked in sweat, feeling gripped, strangled with thoughts, panting, begging for help, craving for the arms and feeling homesick. a person who is tired of struggling and aiming to give life away to criminal thoughts. a person who is trying to find answer to questions someone else left unresolved. a person who feels helpless, hopeless and worthless. i have been there and trust me — it gets better.

had i not poured my heart out to my lord; i wouldn't
have tasted the sweetness of his mercy. trust me, when i
say this — nothing can help you out of despair, nothing
can replace the emptiness in your heart but the
closeness to him. he has a plan for you and you must
put your trust in him. i don't mean that you would be
okay overnight — but your heart will be at ease for
eternity, only if you take a step.

if there is something you must know is that your lord
never leaves your side.
are you feeling down?
isn't there anyone to talk about your problems?
have you been feeling lonely?
trust me, there's nothing that could save you from all
these emotions but him.
you just need to take a step and move forward towards
him.
he will show you why everything that is happening to
you, is happening to you and you will get a direction to
where you need to go.

i know, it is not easy to be patient but it is not difficult
to talk to him and cry.
he is merciful.
he listens.
he sees you.
he is always by your side.

now i know what it means when they say, *"i don't know which is worse, being the one with a broken heart or being the person that breaks the heart."*

now i know it all — i have broken your heart and there's no debate about it.

no 'what-ifs', 'buts', 'could've' or 'should've' can fix it — you wanted me to be happy, turned out you made me the reason of your happiness.

you tell me you've fallen in love with me; you wish you didn't and i wish i could love you the way you love me, i wish i could love you the way you deserve to be loved but this heart of mine is shattered and i only wish i shouldn't have let you touch its pieces.

i don't regret meeting you — i regret that i'm the reason behind your lost smile. i am disappointed that i was breaking your heart while you were trying to fix mine.

now i know what it means when they say, *"there's nothing sadder than meeting the right person at the wrong time."*

i'd ruined my makeup before i could walk down
the aisle and it wasn't something
i ever planned.

it was supposed to be a moment of joy
and all i could do
was cry.

i'm in love with someone
who gave me a stone,
but i was compelled to say yes
to the one who offered me a diamond.

my heart belongs to someone
who was in the crowd,
but fate had me next to a stranger,
to be vowed.

i was helpless because i had a duty to my family
but did, they think twice if i'd ever live happily?

i don't think i'll forgot you ever, no matter how i
shared my bed with a stranger.

i never said anything, kept quiet
and it's the story of my wedding night.

she asked me about you but i lied, like i always do. she
grabbed my phone and looked for your name — but she
is too young to read. she asks me all the time and i
always end up saying that you're busy at work. she
wakes up every morning and hopes to see you at the
breakfast table but i say you've already left for work to
begin with. it is difficult for me to choke back the tears
when she plays music with her fork and spoon, waiting
for you at dinner. she stands by the door over the
weekend and long for you to take her out for a movie,
little does she know that her father is living his own
secret fairy tale. i don't want you to come back for me,
but visit her once and read her a bedtime story. you
must come home and tell her that the king has broken
her heart before any prince would.

he decided to come home tonight - to say the final
goodbye. i can't seem to figure out whose fault it was
and i don't know where it went wrong but i know for a
fact that the world we created together was destroyed
by someone who wasn't a part of it. i remember our
love, commitment and wedding but he has forgotten the
vows and his promises to cherish our marriage forever.
he doesn't hate me, for i know the truth but the love he
once had for me has faded. and for our last dinner as a
couple, he selflessly set the table - served me divorce
paper and offered me a pen. in the end, i've got to keep
the house we lived in together and he took away the
home.

in life, especially during tough times, you'll come across people who will try to shut down your voice — who would want you to apologise for sharing your story, they will try their best to defame you. especially during those times, you must promise to always believe in yourself. their reaction shouldn't change a word in your story because if you do that, you're allowing them to control you. if you listen to those voices — you're giving them the authority to decide who you should be instead of a courageous, kind and beautiful soul that you're meant to be.

hold so much of love in your heart for people, that you never become a source of pain for them. hold so much of kindness in yourself, that you never become a reason for anyone to shed a tear. you should be supportive of their decisions so that they never end up losing sleep. above everything — hold so much of self-respect that you must never let anyone take advantage of you. you should never allow anyone to walk over you. because everyone should be loved by the kindest heart that you have — but not all deserve to stay in it. you should know how to give a piece of yourself to every soul that you touch, but you must not allow anyone to destroy your peace.

if i were to tell something to help you ease this pain, it would be this — "no matter how much you try, what's not meant to be yours, will never be yours." so, let go of the fear and free yourself from unnecessary drama and anxiety. instead, put all your efforts to grow as a person because right now, you're trying to be everything you're not, for people and things that won't matter in the end. you don't have to change yourself to get validation from someone for something that doesn't belong to you. above anything, all you need in this life is the peace of mind and heart. hold on to your truth — let go of the desires that are destroying you and stay strong.

if you think that your faith, your loyalty or the depth of
your love will change the person who could care less
about you right at this moment — there is something
that i must ask you. what kind of love breaks a heart
made of gold? what kind of love hurt you at the places
you did not know existed? tell me what is the need for
you to suffer because of this one person? i know you
know it is not worth it. i can tell that you know it is a
poison to your soul. for one last time, i want you to take
a deep breath, gather all the courage you have and let
go; leave it all behind. i know it will hurt, more than
you can ever anticipate but it will hurt for a while
followed by the lifetime of peace. this love you have in
you for a worthless person is not worth the fight but the
lesson you must take from this toxic person is that your
happiness is worth the fight.

you must know your heart; it doesn't hurt for no reason
— there's always a purpose behind your brokenness.
the pieces of your broken heart are there to pierce
through your soul and turn you into a kind, soft and
compassionate person. they're there to change your
outlook on life and build you into the person you're
meant to be. if i must tell you something — you should
touch these broken pieces and let them hurt you. you
need to let them hurt you until you feel numb. you must
let the sadness in and then let your tears out followed
by the pain. and at times, when your brokenness
doesn't make any sense — hold the pieces in your hand
and watch them slip between your fingers.

do me a favour — detach yourself from toxic people.
distance yourself from every single person who hurts
your self-esteem and damages your smile. please don't
go around someone who makes you question your
existence. i suggest you do whatever it takes to remove
them from your life and this is the best decision you'll
ever take. you deserve happiness, something they don't
have in them to offer.

you must trust those 5 minutes, believe me. those 5 minutes of someone's busy day, that they couldn't bear to text you, says a lot about your place in their lives. those 5 minutes that couldn't be spared out of 24 hours from their day sing a song we don't wish to hear, but those 5 minutes matter a lot. as much busy as it could get, if you are not on anyone's priority list — you must walk away because those 5 minutes make you feel worthless and lower your self-esteem; that ignorance let you down. but here's words of warning, it will only hurt you since they don't have time to acknowledge your presence at the moment and they may take up to 5 days to spare another 5 minutes to notice that you're gone. trust me, you're better off without those 5 minutes.

if you're hurt, broken and feeling empty. if there's pain
at the places you didn't know existed. if you can't sleep
at night and your soul is numb in the morning; this is
for you — you are amazing and i love you. please
know that you're going to be okay and i'm not going to
sugar-coat it. it may take a day or a year but you'll be
okay. you'll be taken care by the love that is coming
your way and you'll hangout with friends you haven't
met yet. i know you are broken but you must know that
the light will enter your soul through the cracked pieces
and your heart will shine like a diamond.

what i concluded over all these years is that the pain of
losing love is more excruciating than the emptiness felt
after having lost love. you know, you would do
everything you can - things you never expected from
yourself; you may cry and choke to death. you can
scream at the top of your lungs, in fact, you may lose
your whole being only to see that nothing works in the
end. it will take months and years of sleepless nights to
understand that nothing can stop what's meant to leave.
if you're living under the impression that hearing your
voice, love would change its mind; let me tell you a
secret. if you see someone walking out of door, please
understand that the more of them has left already.

the biggest lesson i have learnt is this — "people never change." it's strange that we all come with the understanding of mask falling off of people's faces or people showing their true colours. when, in fact, i realised that people never change. people grow. people grow in lies, people grow in fear and anger, people grow in hate — only if you reflect. we get so used to a side of someone that we start to question our relationship with them which changes with their growth. above everything, what i have realised, is this — you can't control how people grow. but for you, i really hope, as difficult as it could get, i hope you choose to grow in love. i hope you gather the courage to walk the path of kindness. i hope you understand how to find right from wrong. i hope you choose to listen to the voice within yourself without the fear of being judged. i hope you choose to grow for good.

if you feel that someone has put you in a situation that you don't deserve, you must do what they don't deserve — forgive them. always choose to forgive people. if they choose to hurt you, you should choose to forgive them. if they come to break you, you must walk away to keep yourself safe. for some, you would be a coward but for yourself, you will end up as a strong person because real strength lies in forgiveness. let them make mistake for themselves and you should fix it for yourself. your decisions define you and their actions reflect them.

"but in the end, it becomes okay", i said.

that's what i love about us humans. we fall and break.
and sometimes, our pieces are shattered across the
room in a dangerous way. we cry and gasp, we think
we won't survive but we do. we get up — brush
ourselves off and try to collect the broken pieces. i
swear, that's what i love about us humans. we possess
the ability to carry on — with or without the missing
pieces.

don't you dare for a second think that you deserve
anything less than happiness. you truly deserve all the
good things in life. it's okay if you're broken and
shattered but it doesn't make you any less. if anything,
remember the last time you had fallen and how you
managed to pick yourself up — think about the last
time you were hurt and how your wounds healed with
time. and if you find yourself alone, go out and look at
the moon — some nights, it's half and other nights, it's
gone only to become whole.

if you ask me, i would advise you to let it go because i know, broken heart doesn't heal overnight. and i won't sugar-coat it — let go of anything isn't as easier as it's spelled but you must take steps; one and then one more. have you been walking on a straight road? try a right turn today. can't you start your day without a cup of coffee? drink a glass of juice in the morning. are you afraid to flaunt your sunglasses? buy two now. healing isn't an event, it's a process. and it shouldn't matter if you're losing people, money or anything you own because i promise you, you'll find yourself in the end. let it go as it wasn't meant to stay and so is your pain. the truth is, the you — you were before this pain has died and once you allow your heart to heal, you'll grow into the person you're meant to be.

you must tell yourself that you deserve nothing less than love and you possess the ability to have more. you should tell yourself that you have the power to bring your dreams to life and you must not let people tell you what you're capable of. you're beautiful and you should smile when you see yourself — you must be your own hero; you have to be your own strength. once you figure out how to love yourself the way you deserve to be loved — you'll understand how to be your own and once you're your own, you'll be everything to everyone around you.

forgive them.

it's not okay that they hurt you, tortured your soul and disturbed the peace of your mind, but you must forgive them. i'm not saying this because i don't care — i'm asking you to do it because you know, at some point in your life, they meant something to you. i know it hurts. you must walk away and pray for them. holding on to the grudge or punishing them won't make any difference to their lives but forgiving them will change your world upside down.

forgive them.

forgive all of them.

don't start disliking someone because they're making a
mistake.

let them fall.
let them crawl.
let them learn and grow.

let them become a better person — the person they're
meant to be.
but stay by their side whenever they should need you.
love them for who they were, for who they are and for
all they are yet to become.
      you must love them till the end.

most often, we try so hard to be everything we're not,
only to impress the person we're in love with to the
extent that we end up forgetting that we're still
someone — whole lot different, had it not been for this
person. we forget our own personalities, our dreams
and happiness, trying to become the best for someone
who doesn't care. how about we try to stay true to
ourselves? what if we focus in achieving our goals and
find peace in not getting the validation from someone
else? how about we be who we are and let someone
love us for who we are? what if we don't lose ourselves
while loving someone? what if we become a better
person while loving someone else?

i'm not here to tell you to love yourself enough to
travel the world, follow your dreams and pursue your
passion. but i want you to promise yourself to love
yourself so much that you let go of toxic people from
your life. i want you to walk away from the partner
who has more sadness than happiness to offer. i want
you to stop inviting relatives who are bringing negative
vibes into your zone. i want you to break your
friendships that are built on mutual hate, gossips and
bitchiness. i don't want you to love yourself so much
that you stop seeing good in people, but i want you to
love yourself enough to see the bad that good people
could bring to you.

i remember when i was growing up, especially during my teenage, i had this idea that few years down the line — i would be free to do anything i want, go anywhere i wish to, say whatever i believe in.

with time i've realised that it's completely opposite — i've come to terms that less is more. there're things that i really want to do but they're not good for my soul, there're people i want to go out with but they don't deserve a second from my watch and there're things i believe in but i no longer see any reason to argue and prove my point.

i don't seek validation from anyone and i don't live to please anyone. i'm who i'm and no one has the right to tell me who i should be.

i know you're in love with this person you thought was your soulmate and i know it hurts not getting the same love in return. i know you opened up to this person you thought would understand and i know it hurts not getting the response that you expected.
but if i ask you this — *'why do you feel the need to be heard by someone who doesn't appreciate your words?'*, what would you tell me?
i know, it's because your heart has built a home in someone who wants to stay barren and trust me, there is nothing in this world that could change it — this person doesn't feel it, you can't make them feel it.
i know it hurts because at some point, it hurt me too. and i want you to know that this gets better — even if you don't have hope, things will change with time.
this person came into your life to break you into pieces and all you need is a little courage to tell yourself that you've had enough. all i want you to do, right at this moment, is to collect all your broken pieces and fix them as much as you can — even if it makes you tired, carry on.
and here's a warning, you can't fix those pieces and become the happy person that you were before you met this person — instead, stitch those pieces with gold and be an artwork made with kindness. that's what you need, that what i need and that's what everyone else around us needs.

december
once meant holidays,
snow and movies.

the month to celebrate, reflect and enjoy.

it's now — no less than a nightmare,
torture, misery
and the end of another year,
                              without you.

had i known that losing you
was only to bring me
back to my *rabb* —

       i'd lose you, a hundred times.

if there's a moment in a day,
when no prayer goes unheard.

i swear –
i seek it every second
to find a way back to you.

i still remember
each word
every phrase
and the echo
of your silence.

i took out my journal
to recall the good
and the bad times.

i saw you there –
on each page that i turned to,
in every sentence that i read.

it's ironic that you were everywhere
in the book
but nowhere around my life.

my little sister had stolen a book from my shelf – it was written by one of my favourite writers. i noticed her as she struggled to read a word. i took the book to help her spell the word – emptiness. *"what does it mean?"*, she asked. *"umm... okay"*, i was silent because i didn't know how to explain it to her. *"it's a feeling."*

"is it a happy feeling?", she asked with excitement. *"no"*, it took me a while to find the right way to explain it to her. *"you know, when you lose your favourite toy, your most favourite – you want this toy with you every second. even when you're not playing with it, you don't want anyone else to have it."*

"you mean sadness", she interrupted. *"no"*, i replied. *"sadness is losing your toy but hopeful enough to believe that you can get another.*
she smiled, looked into my eyes and asked in her curious tone, *"and emptiness?"*

i really hope she would never have to learn what it stands for yet i tried my best to explain, *"emptiness is knowing that there's no toy to replace the lost one."*

This book is entirely the result of a fifty minutes phone call with one of my favourite writers, Huma Adnan.

Huma, I can't put in words how thankful I'm to you for always being there throughout the process of getting this book out.